TEN CARDINAL SECRETS FOR MASTERING THE ART OF NEGOTIATION

Understanding Advanced Negotiation Techniques That Really Work

James Edwards

TABLE OF CONTENTS

INTRODUCTION

Negotiation is an essential component of human relations. It's a part of everyday life, whether we're settling on a corporate agreement, managing relationship affairs, or even just choosing where to eat with friends. Negotiation is an art of persuasion, a process of bargaining excellently, and the secret to reaching win-win agreements.

Acknowledging the value of negotiation is not enough; one must also recognize its revolutionary potential. Negotiation is a vital instrument that enables people to manage problems, settle conflicts, and form coalitions. It serves as a link between contrasting viewpoints, cultures, and areas of interest, promoting cooperation and advancement in a variety of settings.

There is a wealth of knowledge hidden away in the field of negotiation, just waiting to be discovered. As humans who thrive on negotiation, we are always searching for new approaches and perspectives that will improve our abilities and increase our chances of success. 'Ten Cardinal Secrets for Mastering the Art of Negotiation' is all about revealing this hidden wealth of knowledge. You will be mastering negotiation techniques that really work.

Through the pages of this extensive manual, we set off on an adventure that goes beyond traditional bargaining strategies. We will be exploring the fundamental ideas and time-tested tactics that guide fruitful negotiation efforts. All ten of the cardinal secrets are like lights on a route leading to negotiating expertise.

We will examine the subtleties of communication, the act of power, and the complex nature of human conduct as we turn the pages ahead. We'll learn how to handle difficult circumstances with poise, use empathy as a powerful tool, and create long-lasting win-win solutions. These techniques aren't just theoretical ideas; they're also useful insights obtained from actual experiences and the combined knowledge of eminent negotiators.

This book is an essential tool for any individual who desires to thrive in this universe by mastering the art of negotiation. It doesn't matter whether you're experienced or a novice in the art of negotiation, you will discover the cardinal secrets that have the potential to make you a master negotiator. Now, let's set out on this life-changing journey together to discover the Ten Cardinal Secrets for Becoming Experts in Negotiation.

CHAPTER ONE

The Secret of Preparation

A diplomatic game of chess, in which every move matters and preparation is possibly the key determinant of success and loss, is sometimes used to compare negotiation. The proverb "knowledge is power" applies to negotiations as well, highlighting the critical role that careful planning plays in reaching desirable results. This chapter explores the key components of preparation, taking you through the three basic processes of getting ready for a negotiation activity, which includes studying the other party, establishing precise goals and objectives, and developing a well-thought-out negotiation plan.

Investigating Your Counterparty

A successful negotiation starts with having a thorough understanding of your counterparty or opponent in a negotiation activity. Like any communication, having knowledge makes you more confident and enables you to predict their intentions, priorities, and possible strategies. When conducting research about your opponent in a negotiation activity, keep in mind these four important factors:

1. Background and Personality: Learn about their manner of conversation, temperament, and professional qualifications. Are they cooperative or antagonistic? Do they place more importance on fostering relationships or just results?

2. Past Negotiation Experience: Look into their previous negotiation histories, particularly any encounters with people or groups that are comparable to your own. To guide your strategy, find a sequence in their method and results.

3. Interests and motives: Investigate the parties' hidden motives and interests in order to better understand them. What do they want to accomplish? What worries and preferences do they have? Gaining insight into their viewpoint helps you to formulate suggestions and compromises wisely.

4. Constraints and Pressures: Take into account outside variables like time limits, budgetary restrictions, or organizational policies that might affect your counterpart's decision-making. Recognizing their limitations enables you to modify your offers appropriately.

Clearly defining your objectives and goals

In order to successfully handle the difficulties of negotiation, clarity of purpose is crucial. Spend some time precisely defining your goals and objectives before engaging in any negotiations. Think about these four crucial actions:

1. Identify the Perfect Result: Imagine the perfect result you hope to obtain from the discussion. Which demands are you unwilling to budge from, and what compromises are you prepared to make? Clearly defining your criteria gives your negotiating strategy direction.

2. Prioritize Your Goals: Sort your goals into categories based on priority, making a distinction between goals that are necessary, desirable, and unimportant. Your decision-making will be guided by this ranking, which also makes sure that you concentrate your attention on the most important areas of the negotiation.

3. Have Reasonable Expectations: Be reasonable and take into account the advantages and disadvantages of your position in comparison to your opponent. Avoid unduly optimistic or gloomy expectations and instead aim for results that are both impressive and feasible.

4. Create Backup Plans and Results: Have backup plans and results ready in case the negotiations don't go as planned. Having fallback plans helps you stay flexible and solidify your position in the face of shifting conditions.

Formulating an Approach

Now that you have thorough information and well-defined goals, it's time to create a strategy plan that will work for the specifics of the negotiation. The following four techniques can help you create a successful bargaining strategy:

1. Determine Your Leverage Points: Evaluate your origin of leverage, including your resources, expertise, and other possibilities. Diverse elements can yield leverage, including market conditions, timing sensitivity, or distinctive value recommendations.

2. Expect Counterarguments: Based on the results of your investigation, expect possible disagreements and protests from your opponent. Create compelling arguments and proof to successfully address their interests and strengthen your viewpoint.

3. Develop Trust and Rapport: To create a cooperative environment that is favorable to negotiating, give relationship-building and rapport-building with your counterpart top priority. Establishing a foundation of mutual respect, empathy, and intense listening facilitates productive communication and agreement.

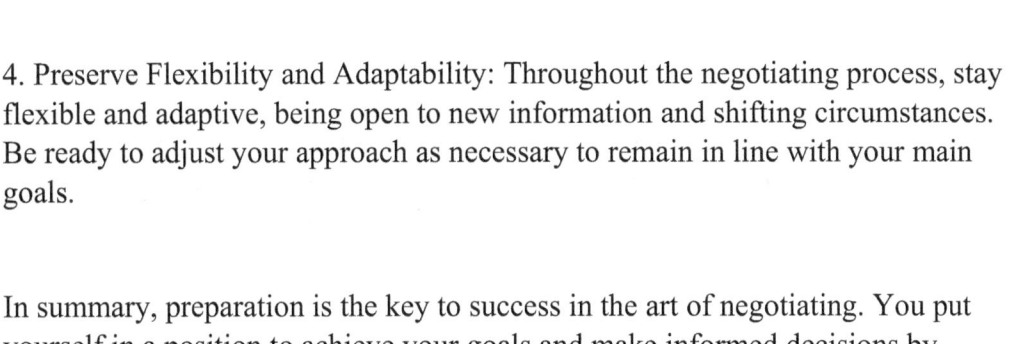

4. Preserve Flexibility and Adaptability: Throughout the negotiating process, stay flexible and adaptive, being open to new information and shifting circumstances. Be ready to adjust your approach as necessary to remain in line with your main goals.

In summary, preparation is the key to success in the art of negotiating. You put yourself in a position to achieve your goals and make informed decisions by devoting time and energy to thoroughly studying your counterpart, establishing precise goals and objectives, and developing a calculated plan of action. It's important for you to acknowledge the fact that negotiation is an active process of cooperation and problem-solving rather than just a debatable transaction. As your helper, extensive preparation allows you to go off on the path to becoming a competent and confident negotiator.

CHAPTER TWO

The Secret of Mastering Communication Skills

Communication is just as important in negotiations as planning and bargaining. Gaining proficiency in communication is essential to successfully handling the intricacies of negotiation. We will explore a number of strategies in this chapter that can improve your ability to communicate and negotiate more effectively. Achieving positive results in negotiations requires a variety of skills, including active listening, rapport-building, and an awareness of the subtleties of both verbal and nonverbal communication.

Four Useful Active Listening Strategies

Active listening is the first step in successful communication. Negotiators far too frequently concentrate just on stating their position without taking the time to fully grasp the opposing side's viewpoint. In order to engage in active listening, one must not only hear what the other person is saying but also understand their hidden motives, worries, and feelings. Here are four useful active listening strategies:

1. Give Your Whole Attention: During a negotiation, give the other side your whole focus. Keep your eyes open, periodically nod to indicate that you understand, and avoid talking over other people.

2. Reflective Listening: To show that you have grasped the other person's viewpoint, paraphrase what they have stated. In addition to demonstrating regard for the speaker, reflective listening helps to confirm understanding.

3. Ask Clarifying Questions: Don't be afraid to inquire in order to learn more about the viewpoints of the other side. Asking clarifying questions might reveal potential areas of bargain and private interests.

4. Empathize: Make an effort to comprehend the feelings that lie at the back of the words. Fostering empathy towards the problems of the other party can facilitate the development of trust and lead to jointly favorable compromise.

Four Relevant Aspects of Potent Verbal and Non-verbal Communication

During negotiations, both verbal and nonverbal suggestions have a big impact on how your message is understood. Gaining proficiency in both areas can improve communication, establish rapport, and exude confidence. The following four elements are crucial to both verbal and nonverbal communication that works:

1. Brief and Simple Communication: Provide your thoughts in a simple and brief manner. Steer clear of jargon and unclear words since they can cause miscommunication.

2. Watch Your Tone: Be mindful of the tone in which you speak. Endeavor to speak in a tone that encourages cooperation over conflict, one that is both assured and courteous.

3. Body Language: You may convey a lot with your body language. To build rapport, keep your posture open, use the right motions, and mimic the other person's body language.

4. Active Participation: Show interest in the discourse by smiling, nodding, and making the right kinds of facial gestures. These nonverbal clues promote conversation and indicate attentiveness.

Four Strategies For Developing A Good Connection During Negotiations

In order to generate confidence and friendliness during negotiations, rapport-building is crucial. People are more prone to work together and discover win-win solutions when they are at ease with one another. Here are four strategies for developing a good connection during negotiations:

1. Find Common Ground: To start creating rapport, look for areas of interest or experiences that you have in common. Finding points of agreement promotes harmony and a sense of connectedness.

2. Active Empathy: Express sincere curiosity about the viewpoint of the other person and show compassion for their worries. Respect their emotions and give credence to what they've experienced.

3. Be Real: Sincerity encourages trust. In order to build rapport, steer clear of scheming strategies and instead be sincere in your conversations.

4. Keep Your Promises and Commitments: Adhere to your word. Developing rapport takes time, and trust must be gradually fostered by upholding integrity.

In summary, effective communication skills are essential for fruitful negotiating results. Negotiators may create meaningful discourse, encourage cooperation, and eventually arrive at win-win solutions that gratify all sides by using active listening skills, gaining proficiency in verbal and nonverbal communication, and developing connections. It's important for you to acknowledge the fact that good communication involves more than just getting your point across; it also entails knowing, relating to, and creating connections that transcend the bargaining table.

CHAPTER THREE

The Secret of Developing Emotional Intelligence

Negotiation is a tactful interplay of emotions as much as a calculated transaction of proposals and counterproposals. The key to an effective negotiation is having the emotional intelligence to recognize, control, and capitalize on the feelings of both parties. We will examine emotional intelligence in this chapter and the manner it can be developed to become an expert negotiator.

Three Relevant Steps to Acknowledging and Controlling Your Emotions for Mastering the Art of Negotiation

In negotiations, emotions are important because they affect relationship dynamics, conversation, and arriving at a decision. The first step to using your emotions as a negotiating tool is to acknowledge and control them. In order to become an expert negotiator, you should follow these three crucial procedures to identify and control your emotions:

1. Self-awareness: Start by becoming aware of your own feelings. Consider your feelings for a moment before engaging in a negotiation. Are you feeling nervous, happy, or maybe even angry? Accept these feelings without passing judgment. You can predict how your state of mind will affect your actions during the negotiating process by being aware of it.

2. Emotional control: In negotiations, emotions may be a strength as well as a possible weakness. While eagerness and excitement can be contagious, unbridled

rage or impatience can sabotage fruitful conversations. When emotions are running high, practice calming tactics like deep breathing, visualization, or excusing yourself for a short break. You can keep your thoughts clear and master your responses by learning to manage your emotions.

3. Empathetic listening: To negotiate effectively, you must do more than just state your own demands and goals; you also need to listen with empathy to the other side in order to comprehend their viewpoints and feelings. To understand the hidden feelings behind someone's statements, you have to pay great attention to their body language, tone of voice, and linguistic signals. Empathy establishes bonds and trust, which pave the way for win-win situations.

Three Relevant Steps to Developing Empathy for Mastering the Art of Negotiation

In order to put yourself in the other party's shoes and understand the situation from their point of view, empathy is required. It is the fundamental component of emotional intelligence in negotiation. Developing empathy improves your capacity for establishing a friendly bond with the other party, successful communication, and problem-solving creativity. The following three actions are crucial to developing empathy in order to become an expert negotiator:

1. Active listening: Engage the speaker completely and show that you genuinely want to hear their point of view. Refrain from interjecting or preparing your reply during the other person's speech. Rather, concentrate on comprehending their innermost desires, emotions, and ideas. Reflective listening strategies that show empathy and promote deeper conversation include summarizing and paraphrasing the words of your counterpart in answer to their questions.

2. Accept Your Counterpart's Viewpoint: Imagine yourself in the other person's shoes to understand their aims, worries, and limitations. Think about how their

experiences, culture, and background have shaped their worldview. You may find points of agreement, work through disagreements, and create solutions that serve the needs of both sides if you comprehend their viewpoint.

3. Emotional validation: Recognize and validate the other person's feelings without essentially accepting their viewpoint. Empathy and understanding are expressed to establish an environment of tolerance and trust that promotes productive communication and teamwork. Validating someone else's feelings does not mean giving in; rather, it means respecting their right to experience their feelings.

Three Relevant Steps to Identifying and Controlling Emotional Triggers for Mastering the Art of Negotiation

Strong emotions are frequently elicited during negotiations due to a variety of variables, including personality conflicts, observed threats, and past experiences. You can remain composed and handle difficult situations with dignity if you can recognize and manage these emotional triggers. In order to become an expert negotiator, you should follow these three crucial stages for recognizing and managing emotional triggers:

1. Trigger awareness: Consider previous discussions or encounters with people that caused intense emotional responses. Determine which circumstances or patterns are likely to elicit strong feelings in you. Being mindful of your triggers helps you prepare coping mechanisms and anticipate them for successful management.

2. Cognitive reframing: Disprove unfavorable perceptions and presumptions that exacerbate emotional responses. Reframe challenges as chances for acquisition of knowledge and development rather than as an unbeatable obstacle. You may proceed towards negotiation with flexibility and optimism in spite of difficulty if you adopt a growth attitude.

3. Stress management: When there is a lot on the line or deadlines are approaching, negotiations can be naturally stressful. Make self-care routines like physical activity, meditation, and time management a priority in order to lower stress and improve emotional toughness. In order to avoid burnout and maintain your focus when negotiating, always remember to keep an optimum harmony in your work and leisure.

In summary, developing emotional intelligence is crucial to being an expert negotiator. It is possible to handle difficult discussions with composure, trust, and empathy if you can identify and manage your emotions, as well as empathize with others. It's important for you to accept the awesome potential of emotional intelligence as a fundamental component of your negotiating arsenal, and observe how it changes both the way you tackle the negotiation process and the results you achieve.

CHAPTER FOUR

The Secret of Understanding and Utilizing Power Dynamics

Each side in a negotiation tries to exert influence over the other in order to get the result they want. Gaining proficiency in the art of negotiation requires a fundamental knowledge of power dynamics and how to utilize it. This chapter will explore the subtleties of power, including how to spot imbalances, use them morally, and create agreements that benefit both parties.

Four Different Types of Power in Negotiation

It's critical to evaluate the power dynamics at play before engaging in any negotiations. There are many ways that power might appear in negotiations. The following four types of power exist in negotiations:

1. Informational Power: This is the result of one party knowing something that the other does not. It might be proprietary statistics, market direction, or intimate knowledge.

2. Resource Power: This is the ability to exercise control over important resources, such as money, technology, or human capital.

3. Positional Power: Originating from positions of hierarchy at institutions of higher learning or in society. Positional power is inherently held by CEOs, managers, and other prominent individuals.

4. Interpersonal Power: This refers to personal attributes like charm, ability to persuade, or subject-matter expertise.

A successful strategy is made possible for negotiators by recognizing these power relations. Identifying your advantages and disadvantages against the opposing party aids in strategy development.

Four Guidelines for Utilizing Power Ethically in Negotiation

In order to negotiate ethically, one must exercise authority sensibly and with regard to the rights and dignity of all parties. Here are four guidelines for using power in an ethical manner during negotiation:

1. Transparency: Avoid lying or exploitation, and be candid about your sources of authority. Transparency creates a more cooperative negotiating atmosphere by establishing trust.

2. Empathy: Seek justice and consideration while acknowledging the power dynamics that can work against the other side. Empathy makes the negotiating process more relatable and encourages more favorable results.

3. Integrity: Respect moral standards and refrain from taking unfair advantage of others or using deceptive methods to obtain an advantage. Having integrity in negotiating improves your trustworthiness and prestige.

4. Empowerment: Provide chances for the other party to be totally engaged in the negotiation process. Allowing the opposing side's voice to be heard in negotiation empowers them, and provides stronger relationships and commitment to better agreement.

Six Potent Strategies for Balancing Power in Negotiations

When there are large disparities in power during negotiation, negotiators can use techniques to eliminate disparities. The following are six effective methods for balancing power during negotiations:

1. Create Alliances: Assemble groups of people or organizations that can support you and give you more clout.

2. Concentrate on Interests: Move the emphasis from positions to basic interests. You can lessen power disparities by identifying common interests and investigating innovative solutions.

3. Create Stronger BATNAs: BATNA is an acronym for Best Alternative to a Negotiated Agreement. In order to lessen reliance on the other side and boost your bargaining power, you should develop various strong BATNAs.

4. Apply Time Pressure: Time is a powerful tool in negotiation. By fabricating deadlines or taking advantage of time restraints, one can force the other party to compromise.

5. Offer Value: To encourage cooperation and balance power disparities in a negotiation activity, render value above the scope of the immediate transaction. This can entail providing more services, knowledge, or resources.

6. Use Negotiation Tactics: To sway opinions and results in your favor, utilize negotiation strategies like framing, anchoring, or reciprocity.

Negotiators can manage power dynamics more skillfully and ethically by utilizing all the tactics stated in this chapter. It will result in more equitable and long-lasting agreements. It's important for you to acknowledge the fact that real negotiation skill is achieved through proficient use of power dynamics to produce win-win agreements rather than by intimidating the opposing side.

CHAPTER FIVE

The Secret of Generating Win-Win Solutions

One side's win is usually seen as the other party's loss in negotiations, which are frequently depicted as a struggle of wills. But there is much more to the art of negotiation than this win-or-lose mentality. In order to become an expert negotiator, one must accept the idea of coming up with win-win solutions where both sides may accomplish their goals and leave happy. The concepts and techniques of cooperative problem-solving, identifying points of agreement, and optimizing value for both sides in negotiation situations are covered in detail in this chapter.

Three Techniques for Developing Cooperative Problem-Solving in Negotiations

Cooperative problem-solving is crucial to generating win-win solutions. Consider negotiation as a cooperative effort to solve shared interests and problems rather than as a competitive sport. A spirit of friendship and trust can be developed by negotiators when they concentrate on common objectives rather than personal benefit. In negotiations, cooperative problem-solving can be established in three ways:

1. Identifying Interests: To begin, ascertain what the parties' fundamental interests are. Examine each side's preferences, demands, and motivations in greater detail than just their stated viewpoints. Through identifying shared interests, negotiators might potentially pinpoint areas of compromise and cooperation.

2. Brainstorming Solutions: To come up with a range of viable answers, promote candid discussion and brainstorming. Promote originality and innovation while looking into options that might be in the best interests of all involved. Ensure a cooperative environment where all suggestions are accepted and assessed according to their compensation.

3. Seeking Mutual Gain: Try to find solutions that take into account the interests and worries of both sides in order to render value for both. Seek out chances to swap favors and engage in advantageous trades. In order to optimize total value and produce win-win situations, negotiators should consider enlarging the beneficial outcome of a negotiation instead of competing over it.

Three Ways of Discovering An Area of Agreement in Negotiations

Discovering an area of agreement is crucial for creating a basis of mutual understanding and compromise, improving cooperative problem-solving. Here are three strategies for discovering an area of agreement in negotiations:

1. Active Listening: To fully comprehend the viewpoint of the other side, engage in active listening. Pay attention to hidden feelings, beliefs, and worries in addition to what is stated. Exhibit empathy and a sincere desire to discover solutions that satisfy the requirements of both sides.

2. Building Rapport: Through constructive dialogue and relationship-building, initiate a bonding connection and trust with your counterpart. Seek out similarities and life experiences that you have in common to help mend divisions and promote cooperation. Developing a good rapport makes it easier to look for alternatives that will benefit both parties.

3. Examining Common Goals: In order to provide stability to the negotiation process, pinpoint common goals and points of compromise. Stress shared objectives and hopes that the two sides can support. Negotiators can facilitate productive communication and agreement by matching interests and ideals.

Three Strategies to Optimize Benefits for Both Parties in Negotiations

The objective of a win-win solution in negotiations is to optimize benefits for all parties involved, not just to come to a consensus. This calls for a calculated strategy that emphasizes finding ways to benefit both parties. In negotiations, there are three methods to maximize value for both sides:

1. Developing Value-Added Solutions: Seek out chances to provide value outside the parameters of the current agreement. Examine unifying negotiation techniques that allow both sides to get beyond their primary expectations. Through the process of recognizing and utilizing complimentary strengths, negotiators can uncover untapped potential and improve general gratification.

2. Sustaining Flexibility: All through the bargaining process, keep your composure and adaptability. Be willing to investigate novel concepts and modify plans in light of fresh knowledge or evolving conditions. Steer clear of dogmatic stances and concentrate on coming up with solutions that accommodate changing interests and demands.

3. Adopting an Approach to Problem-Solving: Instead of approaching negotiations with a competitive perspective, adopt a problem-solving approach. See difficulties and barriers as chances for cooperation and creativity. Through recasting disputes as a challenge that both parties must overcome, negotiators can get beyond obstacles and reach win-win agreements.

Developing win-win solutions is not merely feasible but also necessary for enduring success and the development of lasting relationships when one has mastered the art of negotiating. Negotiators may open up new options and produce enduring value in each negotiation situation by adopting a cooperative problem-solving approach, identifying points of agreement, and optimizing value for both sides.

CHAPTER SIX

The Secret of Negotiating with Confidence

In negotiations, confidence is just as important as procedure. In high-stakes circumstances, it's all about the way you project yourself, the way you manage stress, and the way you get over your fears and anxieties. We'll explore the essential elements of confident negotiation in this chapter, such as expressing confidence, managing pressure, and conquering fear and anxiety.

Six Techniques for Getting Rid of Fear and Anxiety During Negotiations

When faced with negotiation scenarios, fear and worry are normal reactions. It can be extremely crippling to dread rejection, failure, or making the incorrect choice. But it's important to understand that bargaining is a talent that can be developed with practice. These six techniques will help you get over your fear and anxiety during negotiations:

1. Being prepared: You will express more confidence the better prepared you are. Do a lot of research on the subject, comprehend the requirements and goals of the counterparty, and foresee any obstacles or disagreements.

2. Training: To progressively increase your confidence, practice negotiating in informal settings. To improve your skills, role-play with a companion or coworker or take part in simulated negotiations.

3. Positive Visualization: Envision yourself winning the deal. Imagine yourself putting up your case with assurance, responding well to criticism, and coming to a compromise that benefits both parties. Confidence-boosting and anxiety-reducing positive visualization can be helpful.

4. Concentrate on Finding Answers, Not Problems: Rather than lingering on possible issues or mistakes, concentrate on coming up with answers. Embrace a problem-solving mentality and view the negotiating process as a chance to work together to develop original ideas that will satisfy both sides.

5. Deep Breathing and Relaxation Methods: To soothe yourself when you're nervous or agitated, use deep breathing and relaxation methods. Exercises that involve deep breathing can help you feel less anxious and control your heart rate.

6. Challenge Negative Thoughts: Recognize and confront any unfavorable ideas or viewpoints that could be causing you to feel afraid or anxious. Take their place with encouraging words and recollections of your former achievements and assets.

Six Techniques to Express Confidence During a Negotiation

In negotiations, confidence is essential. It affects not just how other people see you but also how you behave and make decisions for yourself. During negotiations, you can convey confidence in the following six ways:

1. Body Language: Be mindful of how you carry yourself. Make eye contact, sit up straight, and stress your remarks with movements. Stay away from dragging and restlessness as these can be signs of insecurity or uneasiness.

2. Voice Tone and Tempo: Use a reasonable tone and tempo while speaking intelligibly and confidently. Speaking too hastily or quietly can give the impression that you lack confidence. Train yourself to get into the attitude of speaking with conviction and assertiveness.

3. Clothes and Appearance: Make sure your attire is suitable for the bargaining situation and that you exuberate confidence and competence. You will have more self-confidence when you dress in a confident manner.

4. Know Your Value: Convince yourself of your value and what you can contribute to the discussion. The foundation of confidence is self-belief in oneself and one's skills. Acknowledge your accomplishments and strengths, and allow them to boost your self-esteem.

5. Be Bold Rather Than Contentious: Confidence is often derived from boldness. Express your demands and priorities in a clear and considerate manner, taking into account the viewpoint of the other person. Steer clear of animosity or contention as these might erode cooperation and trust.

6. Adaptability: When negotiating, exercise flexibility and adaptability. Being adamant or unyielding does not imply confidence. Instead, exude confidence by being receptive to fresh perspectives and prepared to make concessions when needed.

Six Ways of Managing High-Stress Situations in Negotiations

High-stress scenarios are common in negotiations, necessitating calmness and rapid thinking. In negotiations, you can effectively manage pressure in the following six ways:

1. Remain Calm and Focused: Retain your poise in the face of difficulty. Inhale deeply, concentrate on the here and now and admonish yourself of your preferences and aspirations.

2. Practice Active Listening: Pay great attention to the worries and viewpoints of the other person. Respect is shown when you actively listen, and you may learn important information that will improve your negotiating strategy.

3. Remain Adaptable: Have a plan in place to change course when unforeseen events or difficulties arise. Whereas rigidity might impede progress, flexibility lets you change course and come up with new ideas.

4. Excuse Yourself for a Break when Necessary: Don't be afraid to excuse yourself for a little break to regain your composure if the discussion gets too hot or devastating. Taking a quick break can assist you keep your viewpoint and clarity.

5. Ask for Help: If you're experiencing a feeling of stress over a negotiation, do not hesitate to seek assistance. You can ask a coach, mentor, or trustworthy colleague for help. Having someone to guide or reassure you can sometimes be the turning point in handling stressful situations well.

6. Keep the Long-Term Relationship in Mind: It's important to keep in mind that bargaining is more about establishing and preserving a relationship than just getting a deal. Consider the wider picture and aim for results that promote cooperation and trust.

In conclusion, preparation, a positive outlook, and strong communication abilities are all necessary for confident negotiation. You may learn the art of bargaining and produce favorable results by conquering fear and anxiety, exuding confidence, and responding coolly and gracefully to stressful situations. As you continuously apply these techniques, you'll see a gradual increase in your confidence and negotiating skills.

CHAPTER SEVEN

The Secret of Mastering the Art of Persuasion

Persuasion and bargaining play equal roles in negotiations. A strong grasp of persuasion is crucial whether negotiating a price, looking for a good deal, or persuading others to agree with you. This chapter explores a number of strategies to improve your persuasiveness, such as employing influence tactics, employing persuading language, and creating a strong case.

Five Elements of Influence Tactics

1. Reciprocity: According to the principle of reciprocity, people feel compelled to return the favor when you offer them something. Offering little favors or compromise during a negotiation might encourage a reciprocal response and raise the possibility of an agreement.

2. Social Proof: People, particularly in ambiguous circumstances, have a tendency to emulate the behavior of others. To support your argument and provide social proof, use case studies, testimonials, or instances of prior profitable negotiations.

3. Authority: To give your arguments more weight, establish yourself as an authority or draw on the knowledge of others. This could be bringing in experts to back your position, citing studies, or making reference to industry standards.

4. Scarcity: Instilling a sense of urgency or scarcity might persuade people to take immediate action or accept conditions they might not have otherwise. Your proposal's perceived worth might be increased by emphasizing time-sensitive offerings, unique advantages, or insufficient quantity.

5. Consistency: It is human nature for people to stick to their previous declarations, deeds, or promises. By structuring your suggestion in a way that is consistent with the recipient's prior agreements, principles, or convictions, you might encourage agreement.

Five Techniques for Using Words That Persuade

1. Emotional Appeal: Use language that inspires feelings of joy, empathy, or care in order to connect with your counterparts on an emotional level. Your arguments will be stronger if you emphasize the possible advantages or repercussions in words that are relevant to you personally.

2. Power Words: Use strong language that exudes positivity, authority, and assurance. Use words like "unique," "guaranteed," or "life-changing" to give your proposals assurance and appeal.

3. Storytelling: Create tales that support your arguments and speak to the hopes or experiences of your listeners. Stories possess an exceptional capacity to hold readers' interest, inspire empathy, and explain difficult concepts in a way that is relevant.

4. Persuading Questions: Ask persuading questions to help your audience get to the conclusion or viewpoint you want them to see. You can make them more naturally attuned to your perspective by asking them to think about particular points of your argument.

5. Visual Language: Use sensory-engaging, descriptive language to conjure up dramatic mental images. Make your suggestions more real and alluring by drawing the audience's imagination with richly detailed descriptions of results, scenarios, or advantages.

Five Strategies for Initiating a Strong Argument

1. Clarity and Structure: Clearly state your point in a logical fashion, following a well-defined outline that leads naturally from the introduction to the conclusion. Divide difficult concepts into manageable chunks and back up your assertions with relevant data.

2. Recognizing Audience Requirements: Adapt your position to your audience's particular requirements, interests, and worries. Your proposals will be more appealing and relevant if you can show that you know their goals and preferences.

3. Anticipating Objections: Be aware of any possible replies or disagreements and prepare to answer them head-on in your argument. Recognizing and disproving competing arguments builds your position's persuasiveness and establishes your believability.

4. Framing and Framing Effect: Present your case in a way that highlights the merits for your readers. You can sway opinions and decision-making in your favor by centering the conversation around advantages or admirable qualities.

5. Call to Action: Summarize your points with a concise and powerful call to action that encourages your audience to take the desired action. Clearly state what has to happen next and emphasize the advantages of taking certain actions, whether it's accepting terms, committing money, or taking any precise action.

In conclusion, effective negotiating requires a mastery of persuasion. You can improve your capacity to persuade people, obtain good results, and reach advantageous agreements by utilizing influence tactics, persuasive language, and well-crafted arguments. You will be able to negotiate with confidence and grace if you practice and hone these abilities.

CHAPTER EIGHT

The Secret of Handling Stalemate in Negotiations

Seldom does negotiation follow an easy road from beginning to end. You can come across roadblocks and dead ends that could prevent you from moving forward. These obstacles can be caused by a number of things, such as competing interests, obstinacy, or unanticipated events. But becoming an expert negotiator requires not just avoiding dead ends but also knowing how to handle them when they manifest.

Five Typical Difficulties in the Negotiation Process

1. Ego Wars: An often encountered barrier in negotiations is an ego war. Stalemate arises when parties get overly focused on establishing their supremacy or proving they are correct.

2. Inflexibility: Stalemates can result from rigidity in adhering to original positions. There are situations when negotiators get so focused on their demands that they neglect to consider other options.

3. Miscommunication: Ineffective communication or misinterpretations might make it difficult to come to a consensus. Negotiations can easily come to a standstill if requirements and objectives are not expressed clearly.

4. Lack of Trust: Effective negotiating is built on trust. Parties may find it difficult to come to a mutual agreement when they have doubts about one another's honesty or intentions.

5. External Factors: Events or situations outside of the negotiators' control may also cause problems in the process. These can be unanticipated emergencies, obstacles imposed by regulations, or modifications to the market.

Five Strategies for Overcoming Stalemates in Negotiations

1. Active Listening and Empathy: In many cases, stalemates result from a failure to fully comprehend the viewpoint of the other person. This divide can be closed and a more cooperative environment can be created by actively listening and exhibiting empathy.

2. Investigating Interests: Take a closer look at each party's fundamental interests rather than just their positions. You can find innovative solutions that meet the requirements and interests of all parties involved by recognizing common interests or reciprocal needs.

3. Creating Options: When bargaining comes to a standstill, generating alternate solutions helps to break the deadlock. Promote original thought and be receptive to strange concepts that could result in innovations.

4. Looking for Mediation or Facilitation: Using a neutral third party to assist in extremely difficult bargains can help parties discover a productive way to communicate and discover mutual interest.

5. Taking Breaks: Occasionally, taking a brief break from the negotiating table might help with viewpoint and precision. Breaks provide a space for emotions to subside and enable negotiators to reconsider their opinions.

Five Strategies to Keep the Motion of Negotiation Ongoing

1. Concentrate on the Grand Vision: Remind both yourself and the other side of the reasons for obtaining a consensus as well as the ultimate objectives. Maintaining momentum during difficult times can be facilitated by keeping the main goals front and center.

2. Appreciate Little Wins: No matter how tiny, recognize and appreciate small victories. Little victories add up to progress, and success is bred by progress.

3. Remain Adaptable: Breaking through stalemates requires flexibility. In order to keep the bargain going forward, be prepared to modify your strategy, consider fresh approaches, and make compromises as required.

4. Remain Patient: Endurance is frequently put to the test in negotiations. Even when you encounter obstacles, have patience and perseverance. Keep in mind that stalemates are transient challenges that can be solved using persistence.

5. Review Foundational Rules: It could be beneficial to go over the initial foundational rules again if the bargain strays off course. Make expectations clear, reiterate your commitment to polite conversation, and declare your intention to come to a mutually beneficial consensus.

Understanding how to handle stalemates is essential to becoming an expert negotiator. Instead of ignoring them completely, you should view stalemates as chances for improvement and creativity. You may put bargains back on track to produce great results by using practical tactics and keeping an optimistic attitude

CHAPTER NINE

The Secret of Negotiating in Cross-Cultural Circumstances

It can be difficult but also rewarding to negotiate in many cultural circumstances. It necessitates a high degree of cultural intelligence, a thorough comprehension of the subtleties of each relevant culture, and the capacity to modify communication approaches accordingly. This chapter will cover the essential elements of cross-cultural negotiation, including how to manage cultural differences, modify communication tactics, and develop the cultural intelligence required for positive results.

Four Major Ways That Cultural Differences Affect Negotiations

Cultural variations impact negotiations in a big way, affecting everything from decision-making procedures to communication approaches. Prior to engaging in cross-cultural negotiation, it is critical to recognize and honor these distinctions. Four main ways that cultural differences impact negotiating are as follows:

1. Communication Styles: When it comes to communication, diverse cultures have contrasting choices. Simplicity and firmness may be valued more highly in some cultures than wordiness and subtlety in others. For instance, whereas establishing rapport and upholding harmony are valued more highly in many Asian cultures, negotiators in Western cultures frequently prefer to get right to the point.

2. Decision-Making Processes: There are also notable cultural differences in how people approach making decisions. Decisions are made in specified order in certain

societies, with those in positions of authority having the last word. In others, choices are made by means of group discussion and concurrence building. Comprehending the decision-making process within a specific culture might aid negotiators in maneuvering through the process more skillfully.

3. Time Orientation: There are wide cultural differences in how people view time. While some cultures follow time limits and agendas to the letter, others are more laid back.

4. Approach Toward Risk and Ambiguity: Different cultures have different approaches toward risk; some value taking calculated risks, while others prefer to avoid ambiguity. These approaches can have an impact on negotiating tactics. Negotiators need to be conscious of these variations and modify their strategy appropriately.

Four Major Ways of Adapting Communication Styles to Different Cultures for Effective Negotiation

When negotiating between cultures, it is imperative to modify one's communication techniques. Talking the language is simply one aspect of successful communication; another is being aware of cultural quirks and modifying one's communication style proportionately. For successful negotiating, there are four main approaches to modifying communication styles to fit various cultural contexts:

1. Active Listening: Although it is a common negotiation skill, different cultures may have different ways of putting it into practice. Silence can be taken as a sign of displeasure or lack of agreement depending on the culture. In some, it is regarded as a symbol of thoughtfulness and introspection. It is necessary to comprehend these cultural clues in order to communicate effectively.

2. Nonverbal Communication: Body language and facial expressions are examples of nonverbal clues that might have diverse cultural connotations. For instance, making eye-to-eye contact may be perceived as aggressive or insulting in other cultures, even though it is frequently considered an expression of sincerity and confidence in Western societies. Negotiations can go more smoothly if these distinctions are kept in mind.

3. Language Use: The choice and ability of language can also influence a negotiation. Even though it's frequently said that English is the dialect of business, not all negotiators will speak it well. In these situations, communicating and establishing rapport might be facilitated by the use of interpreters or reworded knowledge.

4. Cultural Sensitivity: When changing communication patterns, cultural sensitivity is the most important factor to consider. Respecting cultural conventions and customs establishes rapport and empathy, which are essential for productive discussions.

Four Major Ways of Developing Cultural Intelligence for Effective Negotiation

As a crucial skill for negotiators working in cross-cultural settings, cultural intelligence refers to the capacity to communicate and collaborate with individuals from diverse cultural backgrounds. Acquiring cultural intelligence entails learning about many cultures, acknowledging one's own cultural prejudices, and modifying behavior appropriately. Here are four major ways of developing cultural intelligence for effective negotiation:

1. Cultural Awareness: Acquiring knowledge about the principles, mindset, and communication modalities of various cultures is a necessary part of developing

cultural awareness. Cross-cultural training courses, continuous introspection, and cultural engagement encounters can help achieve this.

2. Empathy and Perspective-Taking: In cross-cultural discussions, when cultural differences may cause conflicts or disputes, empathy is crucial for comprehending and accepting others' viewpoints. By using the skill of adopting others' viewpoints or perspective-taking techniques, negotiators can develop respect and understanding between parties by learning to see things from their perspective.

3. Resilience and Flexibility: In cross-cultural negotiations, resilience and flexibility are critical abilities. Negotiators can negotiate cultural differences and arrive at win-win solutions by being receptive to new ideas, willing to make concessions, and mindful of cultural clues.

4. Ongoing Education and Development: Developing cultural intelligence is a lifelong process that calls for constant education and development. It is recommended that negotiators solicit criticism, engage in introspection, and proactively pursue avenues to augment their cultural competency.

In summary, developing cultural intelligence, adjusting communication methods, and comprehending cultural differences are all necessary for successful cross-cultural negotiation. Negotiators can break through cultural limitations, forge closer bonds with others, and accomplish favorable results in the international marketplace by honing these abilities.

CHAPTER TEN

The Secret of Acquiring Knowledge from Every Negotiation

In addition to being a debatable exchange, negotiation is an active process that involves bargain, persuasion, and conversation. Whether the negotiation is successful or not, all parties involved can learn a great deal from it. It takes more than just getting what you want out of a negotiation to become an expert; you also need to keep acquiring knowledge and improving with every negotiation. This chapter delves into the significance of contemplation, ongoing enhancement, absorbing wisdom from each negotiation, and utilizing knowledge in subsequent negotiations.

How to Contemplate Your Negotiation Skills Continually for Improvement

The foundation for improving one's negotiation abilities is contemplation. Spend some time thinking back on the negotiations and their results after each one. Think back on what went well, what could have been done better, and any unforeseen difficulties that developed. You can gain important lessons for future communication by thinking back on both your personal performance and the mechanics of the negotiation.

Consider the following: Did I express my preferences and concerns clearly? How carefully did I hear what the other person had to say? Were there any chances for cooperation or agreement lost? Were emotions involved in the negotiation, and in that case, to what extent? Which tactics worked best and which didn't work as well?

You can pinpoint areas that need work by assessing both the negotiation and your display intensely. This contemplation establishes the groundwork for ongoing negotiation skill development.

Five Ways of Absorbing Wisdom from Every Negotiation

No matter how the negotiation turns out, there is always wisdom to glean. Make the effort to analyze both successful and bad negotiations in order to assimilate necessary wisdom. Investigate the fundamental causes that impacted the result by looking past the obvious consequences. When attempting to get insight from each negotiation, take into account the following five factors:

1. Look for patterns: Do certain issues or themes come up again in several negotiations?

2. Assess tactics: Determine the efficacy of the various strategies and tactics used in negotiations.

3. Gain an understanding of the Counterparty: Consider the goals, priorities, and modes of communication of the counterparty.

4. Learn from Errors: Recognize your errors and take steps to prevent them from happening again when negotiating.

5. Celebrate Accomplishments: Acknowledge and duplicate effective strategies or results.

Being receptive to criticism and willing to reflect on oneself are prerequisites for gleaning wisdom from negotiations. Accept both the achievements and the setbacks as chances for development and education.

Four Strategies for Applying the Knowledge You Acquired from Negotiations to Future Negotiations

The real benefit of taking what you've learned from each negotiation is using it to inform future exchanges. Gaining a more profound comprehension of your advantages, disadvantages, and the implications of negotiations will enable you to address future discussions with increased assurance and efficacy. The following four tactics can help you use the knowledge you gained during negotiations in subsequent ones:

1. Create a plan: Determine how you will address future discussions based on your contemplations and the wisdom you acquired. Determine your areas of strength and weakness to maximize your strengths and improve on your weaknesses.

2. Adapt and innovate: When it comes to negotiating, stay resilient and flexible. Apply fresh strategies and methods that are informed by your observations and encounters.

3. Create connections: Put your energy into getting to know the other person and earning their trust. To promote cooperation and win-win outcomes, make use of your comprehension of their priorities and driving forces.

4. Remain strong: There will inevitably be obstacles and setbacks during negotiating. Make use of the knowledge and experiences you've gained from the past to overcome challenges with tenacity and resolve.

You can become an expert in the art of negotiating by continuously improving your techniques and putting the knowledge you've learned from each encounter to use. Keep in mind that successful negotiating involves developing rapport, promoting understanding, and adding value for all sides. It's not simply about getting a bargain. Accept every negotiation as a chance to improve, gain knowledge, and become an expert negotiator.

CONCLUSION

This book offers a thorough manual for anyone who wants to improve their negotiating abilities and succeed in a variety of life situations. We've learned priceless lessons along the way that can completely change the way we negotiate in all of our interactions — personal, professional, and business.

In a nutshell, the ten cardinal secrets to mastering the art of negotiation can be summed up in the following sentences. Prepare thoroughly by learning about and comprehending the needs, objectives, and motivations of your counterpart. Maintaining concentration during negotiations can be achieved by clearly picturing and focusing on your goals. Actively listening to your opponent in order to establish rapport and comprehend their point of view. Identifying and skillfully controlling emotions to keep control and get through difficult circumstances. Acquiring flexibility and being willing to consider many approaches in order to get to win-win accords. Using your tone, body language, and manner to project confidence will help you come off as credible and trustworthy. By carefully being silent, you can persuade your opponent to divulge important information or change their mind. Creating a cooperative atmosphere based on honesty and integrity in order to cultivate long-term partnerships. Aiming for results that will satisfy and mean something to both sides, so encourages goodwill and further collaboration. Recognizing when a negotiation is unproductive and being prepared to end it in order to safeguard your interests.

Finally, keep in mind that developing your negotiating skills is an ongoing effort. Put these cardinal secrets into practice, think back on your encounters, and gradually improve your strategy. Accept every negotiation as a chance for development and education. Through commitment and persistence, you will develop into an expert negotiator who can skillfully and confidently handle any situation.

www.ingramcontent.com/pod-product-compliance
Lightning Source LLC
Chambersburg PA
CBHW070448290526
45791CB00005B/2098